GOSPEL OF JOHN

JESUS THE GOD / MAN

MIKE MAZZALONGO

STUDENT WORKBOOK

BIBLETALK.TV

**DOWNLOAD
OUR APP**

Table of Contents

Gospel of John
Jesus the God/Man

Mike Mazzalongo

This study of the fourth gospel by John the Apostle lays out the case for Jesus' dynamic nature as the God/Man and the various reactions people had when confronted by this amazing reality.

bibletalk.tv/gospel-of-john

1. Prologue

In the opening verses of chapter one John goes back before the beginning of time to introduce Jesus and His relationship to God. (John 1:1-18)

_____

_____

Intro - Background of the Book of John

_____

_____

John, The Man:

- Mark 1:20 _____

- Matthew 4:21-22 _____

- Matthew 17:1 _____

- Luke 9:54 _____

- John 19:26-27 _____

- Acts 3:1 _____

Purpose of the Gospel of John

_____

_____

1. Jesus is presented as _____

2. The rise and development of _____

3. The rise and development of _____

Outline

1. Prologue – 1:1-18 _____

_____

2. Proof through Ministry – 1:19-12:50 _____

_____

3. Proof through Death and Resurrection 13:1 – 21:25 _____

_____

Prologue – 1:1-18

_____

_____

Logos/Word _____

_____

_____

Jews _____

_____

_____

Gentiles _____

_____

_____

1:1 –

    "in the Beginning..." _____

_____

_____

    - "...was the word..." _____

_____

_____

    - "...and the Word was with God..." _____

_____

_____

    - "...and the Word was God." _____

_____

_____

1:2 – John "connects" Jesus and the Word. _____

_____

_____

1:3 _____

_____

1:4-5 _____

_____

God is the Word in eternity _____

_____

_____

The Word is Jesus creating the universe _____

_____

_____

Jesus is the life bringing light to the world _____

_____

_____

1:6-8 – John the Baptist _____

_____

_____

1:9-11 – Reviews vs. 5 _____

_____

_____

1:12-13 – The Gospel in capsule form _____

_____

_____

1:14 –

Becoming "flesh" is the incarnation: _____

_____

_____

From God/Word…To Word/Jesus…To Jesus/Man _____

_____

_____

The only begotten from the Father _____

_____

_____

1:15 _____

_____

_____

1:16 _____

_____

_____

1:17 – Moses and the Law/Jesus and Grace _____

_____

_____

1:18 _____

_____

Summary

Three Witnesses:

1. _____

_____

_____

_____

2. _____

_____

_____

_____

3. _____

_____

_____

_____

2. John's Witness

John picks up the earthly history of Jesus' ministry with a description of John the Baptist's work in preparing the people for the arrival of the Messiah. (John 1:19-34)

_____

_____

Intro - The three "strands" of John's gospel:

Strand #1 _____

_____

Strand #2 _____

_____

Strand #3 _____

_____

John the Baptist

John and his ministry were a fulfillment of prophecy concerning the Messiah. (Malachi 3:1-3)

_____

_____

_____

Reaction of a Believer

1:19 _____

_____

1:20-21 – Three Questions:

Are you the _____?

Are you _____?

Are you the _____?

_____

_____

1:22 _____

_____

1:23 – John answers that he is two things:

_____

_____

1:24 _____

_____

1:25 _____

_____

When we're challenged with truth, there are only three ways to respond:

Become _____.

Rationalize _____.

Submit _____.

1:26-28 _____

_____

1:29-34 – John's "witness" contains four elements.

The _____ of Christ's coming – vs. 29

The _____ of the One to come – vs. 30

The _____ of His ministry – vs. 31

The _____ of His ministry – vs. 32-34

Summary

So we have our first episode where we observe all three strands:

Jesus the God/Man _____

Disbelief _____

Belief _____

3. The Pattern of Witness

In this lesson we explore the pattern of witness used by the apostle John, John the Baptist, and Jesus Himself to recruit disciples. (John 1:35-51)

_____

_____

Intro – Review - John uses three narrative strands:

1. _____

2. _____

3. _____

The Prologue _____

_____

_____

First Character and Witness – John the Baptist _____

_____

_____

Witness – Background

The "power of witness" _____

_____

1:35-51 is a pattern for witness evangelism _____

_____

The Greek word Martus / Martur – Martyr _____

_____

The Pattern and Power of Witness

- John 1:1-18 is John's witness of Christ.
- John 1:19-34 is the Baptist's witness of Christ.
- John 1:35-51

1:35-37 – How do witnesses become witnesses? _____
_____

1:38-39 – What did Jesus do with these two? _____
_____

1:40-42 – What does Andrew do? _____
_____

Note the pattern or cycle:

1. _____
_____

2. _____
_____

3. _____
_____

4. _____
_____

God – Christ – John – Disciples – Disciples

1:43-46 – The same cycle repeated. _____
_____
_____

1:47-49 – John gives more details concerning Jesus' witness and the Disciples reaction.

1. _____
_____

2. _____
_____

1:50-51 – Truly, truly means _____
_____
_____

Nathaniel _____

_____

    Heavens Opening Up _____

_____

    Son of Man _____

_____

Christian Witness

Comments about Christian witnessing and its importance.

1. Each of us owes _____

_____

_____

    Not every witness is alike _____

    We are each _____

_____

2. The subject of our witness is _____

_____

_____

Our basic witness is not: _____

_____

    Our witness is that Jesus is _____ and the _____. _____

_____

_____

    The purpose of our witness is to _____.

_____

_____

3. Our witness should be confirmed by our _____

_____

_____

Matthew 5:16 _____

_____

Biblical witnesses often forfeited their lives in order to confirm their witness. _____

_____

_____

Summary

True maturity comes in Christ when we complete the cycle of witnessing. _____

_____

_____

_____

People fail to witness in several ways:

A. No direct witness _____

_____

_____

B. No confirmation _____

_____

_____

We will never see the power of God working in our lives if we _____

_____

_____

_____

4. Miracle at Cana

In this lesson, we witness the first of Jesus' amazing miracles that establish His God/Man nature. (John 2:1-12)

_____

_____

The Wedding at Cana – 2:1-12

_____

_____

Jesus is in the northern part of Israel.

_____

_____

Background on Jewish wedding feasts in Biblical times.

_____

_____

_____

John 2:1-3 _____

_____

2:4-5 _____

_____

2:6-8 _____

_____

1. His answer reveals His awareness and control. _____

_____

_____

2:9-10 – The host compliments the wine. _____

_____

_____

2. Comments on the miracle. _____

_____

_____

A. The _____ of it.

_____

_____

B. The _____ of it.

_____

_____

The "debate" over wine. _____

_____

_____

Jesus took moments to produce what normally took months. _____

_____

_____

The key to this passage is… _____

_____

_____

John 2:11 _____

_____

John notes that this was His first "sign" _____

_____

_____

5. The Cleansing of the Temple

In this lesson, we will examine the layout of the Temple in Jerusalem and the reasons why Jesus expelled the money changers and merchants. (John 2:13-25)

_____

_____

Now that Jesus has taken a first step into public ministry, He will go to Jerusalem for a more

dynamic demonstration of His authority and power.

_____

_____

John 2:13-14 _____

_____

_____

_____

The court of the Gentiles was symbolically the entrance court where all nations could enter

and pray together. _____

_____

_____

Temple tax was collected from everyone 20 years and over. _____

_____

_____

2:15-17 – Jesus forces these merchants and their good out of the Temple area. _____

_____

_____

_____

2:18-22 – The Jews had established many customs in their religion with the disclaimer that said, "until Elias/Elijah comes." _____

_____

_____

_____

Jesus gives them a sign, but one that will serve to condemn them in the end. _____

_____

_____

_____

_____

2:23-25 – Many believed his miracles but were not ready to accept His teaching.

_____

_____

_____

_____

Summary

Note the different strands mentioned in these passages _____

_____

_____

_____

_____

_____

_____

6. Changed by Faith

Nicodemus gains 3 important insights concerning the change needed in order to enter into the kingdom of God. (John 3:1-16)

_____

_____

Intro – Jesus and Nicodemus, and the necessary changes to enter the kingdom.

_____

_____

_____

Text – John 3:1-16

3:1-2 – Nicodemus comes after dark out of fear.

_____

_____

_____

_____

He has faith, but it is limited. _____

_____

_____

Kingdom of God = God's will being done. _____

_____

_____

Nicodemus himself had to be changed. _____

_____

_____

3:4 – Nicodemus pursues the question of "change." _____

_____

_____

       Look at Nicodemus' attitude. _____

       _____

       _____

3:5 – Nicodemus' humility leads to knowledge _____

_____

_____

He receives two important insights:

1. As a scholar _____

    _____

    _____

2. As a contemporary _____

    _____

    _____

3:6 _____

_____

_____

3:7-8 – Nicodemus is amazed. _____

_____

_____

3:9 _____

_____

_____

3:10-11 – Jesus points out that it isn't intelligence that is lacking, it is _____

_____

_____

3:12-13 – Jesus explains that you need faith to understand spiritual things. _____

_____

_____

3:12-15 – Parallel with Numbers 21:9 event. _____

_____

_____

3:16 _____

_____

_____

_____

Summary

If you were in Nicodemus' place here are some things you would have learned.

1. No one goes to heaven without _____.

_____

_____

_____

2. The change takes place _____.

    A. Powered _____

_____

_____

_____

_____

B. Based _____

_____

_____

_____

C. Happens _____

_____

_____

_____

_____

3. Jesus is _____

_____

_____

_____

_____

Epilogue

Nicodemus' life changed.

_____

_____

_____

_____

_____

_____

_____

7. The Mystery Revealed

In this lesson Mike summarizes God's plan of salvation kept secret from angels and prophets. (John 3:17-21)

_____

_____

Intro – A review of Jesus' discussion with Nicodemus and the revelation of the "mystery of the gospel."

_____

_____

God's Plan: Salvation by Faith

The major religions and their views on salvation.

Near Eastern Religions

Judaism – 1400 BC _____

_____

Zoroastrianism – 600 BC _____

_____

Islam – 600 AD – 5 Pillars

1. _____

2. _____

3. _____

4. _____

5. _____

Christianity – 30 AD _____

_____

_____

_____

Eastern Religions

Hinduism – Oldest _____

_____

Jainism – 500 BC _____

_____

Sikhism – 1400 AD _____

_____

Far Eastern Religions

Confucianism – 500 BC _____

_____

Shinto (Japan) _____

_____

Buddhism – 500 BC _____

_____

Taoism – 600 BC _____

_____

Miscellaneous Religions

Animism _____

_____

Naturalism – 1700 AD _____

_____

_____

_____

11 out of 12 of these religions have only three ways to obtain salvation:

    1. _____

    2. _____

    3. _____

They only promise two forms of salvation:

    1. _____

    2. _____

God's Religion and Salvation

Spiritual principles at work in Numbers 21:4-9:

    1. _____

    2. _____

    3. _____

In Numbers 21:4-9:

- The disobedience was _____

- The penalty was _____

- The atonement was _____

- The response was _____

_____

_____

In John 3:15:

- The sins are _____

- The penalty is _____

- The atonement is _____

- The response is _____

The salvation of God is not a cycle of life to oblivion or physical paradise, it is _____

_____

_____

The way to God's salvation is not the various "human" efforts prescribed by man-made religions.

_____

_____

_____

God's way is through _____

_____

_____

Other religions fail because they don't provide mankind with an _____

_____

_____

Man's Response to God's Plan – vs. 17-21

Vs. 17 _____

Vs. 18 _____

Vs. 19 _____

Vs. 20 _____

Vs. 21 _____

_____

_____

_____

God's justice is right!

- Those who accept the light will _____ in it.

- Those who refuse will remain in the _____.

_____

_____

_____

_____

8. John's Final Witness

John describes John the Baptist's reaction to the growth of Jesus' ministry and the decline of his own. (John 3:22-36)

_____

_____

Intro – The usual cycle of belief and disbelief continues to be seen as Jesus' ministry grows and overtakes John the Baptist's Ministry.

_____

_____

Baptism

John 3:22 _____

_____

Baptism – The Word _____

_____

Baptism – The Practice _____

_____

- Priests – John 2:6
- John the Baptist – Matthew 3:11
- Baptism of Suffering – Mark 10:38
- Baptism of Fire – Matthew 3:11; I Corinthians 3:13
- Baptism with/in the Holy Spirit – John 1:33

Before His coming _____

During His ministry _____

After His resurrection _____

Acts 2:1-4 _____

_____

Acts 2:38 _____

_____

II Timothy 3:16 _____

_____

Baptism of Jesus – Mark 16:16

- Authorized _____

- Required _____

- Remains _____

John 3:23-26 _____

_____

John's Last Witness

A. John's witness about _____ 3:27-28.

_____

_____

B. John's witness about _____ 3:29-30.

_____

_____

C. John's witness about _____ 3:31-36.

_____

_____

Epilogue – 4:1-3

_____

_____

_____

_____

9. The Woman at the Well

Jesus uses an encounter with the woman at the well in Samaria to reveal His true identity. (John 4:1-42)

_____

_____

Intro – John follows three themes in describing Jesus as the God/Man:

1. _____

2. _____

3. _____

The Journey – 4:1-6:

Background – Samaria _____

_____

John 4:1-4 _____

_____

4:5-6 – Samaria had once been capital of the Northern Kingdom _____

_____

Jews hated Samaritans because: _____

_____

_____

Jesus and the Woman at the Well – vs. 7-26

4:7-8 – John shows Jesus as very human _____

_____

_____

4:9 – _____

_____

4:10 – Jesus now responds as the Son of God _____

_____

_____

Living Water – Jeremiah 2:13 _____

_____

_____

4:11-12 – Her response is similar to that of Nicodemus _____

_____

_____

4:13-14 – Jesus explains difference between natural and "living" water.

     1. _____

     2. _____

     3. _____

4:15 – The woman asks two questions:

1. _____

2. _____

4:16-18 – Jesus delves into her personal life. _____

_____

_____

_____

4:19-20 – The woman goes from curiosity to preliminary faith. _____

_____

_____

_____

4:21-24 – Jesus explains three things about worship:

1. _____

2. _____

3. _____

God is spiritual and so it' the spiritual reality behind the physical reality that counts.

A. Singing is physical _____

_____

_____

B. Bread and wine are physical _____

_____

_____

C. Money is physical _____

_____

_____

D. Words are physical _____

_____

_____

4:25-26 – The woman is on the verge of faith. _____

_____

_____

Dialogue with the Apostles – vs. 27-35

The Apostles are surprised.

_____

_____

4:27-30 _____

_____

_____

Vs. 31-38 – Jesus speaks to them on a spiritual level:

1. _____
2. _____
3. _____
4. _____

The Woman's Witness – vs. 39-42

The woman shared her encounter with Jesus. _____

_____

_____

4:39 _____

_____

_____

4:40-42 – Her witness affected others:

1. _____

_____

2. _____

_____

3. _____

_____

4. _____

_____

10. Jesus' Method of Personal Evangelism

In the encounter with the woman at the well, Jesus demonstrates His method of multiplication evangelism.

_____

_____

Intro – Review theme lines:

1. _____

2. _____

3. _____

This same passage demonstrates Jesus' approach to personal evangelism. _____

_____

_____

Personal Evangelism

Evangelism is the process of sharing the precious salvation we've received with others.

_____

_____

Multiplication System

Math rules _____

_____

_____

    (Checkerboard and Sugar) _____

    _____

    _____

Now pretend that these marbles are Christian converts! _____

_____

_____

_____

Making and Multiplying Disciples

John 4:1-41 demonstrates seven steps in making and multiplying disciples:

Step #1 _____

_____

_____

Contact is anytime when _____

_____

_____

Note that He allowed no barriers between Him and _____.

_____

_____

Step #2 _____

_____

_____

Challenge happens when you leave the boundaries of

normal conversations to _____.

_____

_____

He challenged her with _____ _____

_____

_____

Step #3 _____

_____

_____

34

The challenge needs to be backed up with the tangible _____ of Christian life.

_____

_____

Step #4 _____

_____

_____

The call comes in many forms but it is always to follow _____.

_____

_____

Step #5 _____

_____

_____

The time is different but eventually everyone must _____.

_____

_____

We fail by going to extremes.

    A. Never ask _____

    B. Ask too quickly _____

Step #6 _____

_____

_____

The new convert is trained to act and speak like a disciple.

_____

_____

The burden rests with the _____.

_____

_____

Step #7 _____

_____

_____

She could have added, but in going to the men of the city, she _____,

_____

_____

Summary

_____

_____

Why don't we multiply?

    A. _____

    B. _____

In the multiplication system:

Everyone is a potential _____

We always look for an opportunity to _____

We are able to supply _____

We are not afraid to go for _____

The church is equipped to _____

Are we ready for the risk? _____

11. Taking God at His Word

In this lesson Jesus teaches that the essence of faith is believing God based on His Word and not relying on "signs" or miracles. (John 4:42-54)

_____

_____

Intro – Review three themes:

1. _____

2. _____

3. _____

Three themes but one objective – John 20:30-31 _____

_____

_____

John had <u>us</u> in mind when he wrote. _____

_____

_____

Proof of Divinity

Jesus' approach to revealing His identity:

1. The _____ concerning Jesus.

2. The _____ of Jesus

3. The _____ of Jesus

_____

_____

We have a cycle within a cycle:

A. Large cycle _____

_____

_____

_____

B. Small cycle _____

_____

_____

_____

Jesus Returns Home – 4:43-45

Jesus' life so far:

- Born _____

- Travel _____

- Grown Man _____

- Baptism _____

- 40 Days _____

- Cana _____

- Jerusalem _____

- Preaches _____

- Returns _____

- Samaria _____

_____

_____

4:43-45 – No honor in your hometown _____

_____

_____

The People Seek Signs – 4:46-48

4:46-47 _____

_____

_____

_____

4:48 – Reasons for Jesus' answer to the official.

1. Motivation _____

2. Faith _____

_____

_____

Mature faith is that which relies on the <u>Word</u> of the Lord. _____

_____

_____

_____

The Miracle – 4:49-52

4:49-52 – Jesus challenges the official _____

_____

_____

_____

Note the evangelism system in action here. _____

_____

_____

_____

The System in Complete – 4:53-54

We see all seven steps of Jesus' evangelism method in His dealership with this man:

1. Contact _____

2. Challenge _____

3. Proof _____

4. Call _____

5. Conversion _____

6. Consecration _____

7. Multiplication _____

Summary

Some key lessons from this passage:

1. Jesus demonstrates _____

_____

_____

    A. _____

    B. _____

    C. _____

    D. _____

2. The point of the book is _____

_____

_____

_____

_____

3. Mature faith is that which _____

_____

_____

_____

_____

_____

_____

_____

12. Six Ways to Lose Your Soul

In His response to the attacks by the Pharisees Jesus describes a variety of ways to lose one's soul. Each of these being demonstrated by the Jewish leaders who were opposing Him. (John 5:1-47)

_____

_____

Intro – John's book has a cyclical nature:

Large Cycle _____

Smaller Cycle _____

The Miracle – 5:1-9

Vs. 1-4 _____

_____

Vs. 5-9 _____

_____

The Conflict – vs. 9-15

Jesus performed his miracle on the "Sabbath"

_____

_____

     Genesis 2:1-3 _____

     Exodus 13-17; 34:21 _____

     _____

     _____

4 B.C. _____

_____

_____

5:10 _____

_____

5:11 _____

_____

5:12-13 _____

_____

5:14-15 – Jesus deals with both the physical and the spiritual health of the man.

_____

_____

The Accusations – vs. 16-18

The miracles bring both new contacts and new adversaries.

Vs. 16 _____

Vs. 17 _____

Vs. 18 _____

_____

Six Ways to Lose One's Soul – vs. 19-47

1. _____ vs. 19-23

_____

_____

They denounced Him for doing the very thing He was sent to do. _____

_____

_____

2. _____ vs. 24-30

_____

_____

Their judgment of Him showed how unprepared they were for their own judgment.

_____

_____

3. _____ vs. 31-38

_____

_____

Jesus reveals the hardness of their own hearts _____

_____

_____

Our hard heartedness can cause us to lose our souls as well. _____

_____

_____

4. _____ vs. 39-40

_____

_____

They had knowledge but no insight. _____

_____

_____

We also miss the connection these men ignored as well. _____

_____

_____

5. _____ vs. 41-44

_____

_____

They didn't honor Him because He made them angry by not honoring them. _____

_____

_____

6. _____ vs. 45-47

_____

_____

Jesus didn't have to accuse them; something else had already done that. _____

_____

_____

They stood condemned because their actions belied their words. _____

_____

_____

Summary

Jesus demonstrates His power by pronouncing judgment on His opponents. _____

_____

_____

They were guilty and at risk because:

1. _____
2. _____
3. _____
4. _____
5. _____
6. _____

How does this lesson transfer to us?

A. If you're not a Christian _____

_____

B. If you're not faithful as a Christian _____

_____

C. If you are a faithful Christian _____

_____

13. Two Promises from Jesus

In chapter 6 of John, Jesus performs mighty miracles to prove His divine nature and makes two important promises to His followers. (John 6:1-40)

_____

_____

Intro – Review John so far. _____

_____

The cyclical pattern:

    Cycle of Revelation _____

_____

    Cycle of Events _____

_____

    Pattern of Evangelism _____

_____

The First Miracle – 6:1-15

6:1-13 – The Miracle _____

_____

_____

6:14-15 – The Reaction _____

_____

_____

Jesus refuses them for three reasons:

    Only God _____

_____

    They saw Him as _____

_____

    They wanted _____

_____

The Second Miracle – vs. 16-36

1. The Miracle – vs. 16-21 _____
_____

2. Jesus declares His divinity – vs. 22-27 _____
_____
_____

3. Reaction of the Crowd – vs. 28 _____
_____
_____

4. Jesus' Response – vs. 29 _____
_____
_____

5. The Crowd's Response – vs. 30-31 _____
_____
_____

6. Jesus' Response – vs. 32-33 _____
_____
_____

7. The Crowd's Response – vs. 34 _____
_____
_____

8. Jesus declares His divinity – vs. 35 _____
_____
_____

Throughout the dialogue He has declared His divinity to them in various ways.

- Messiah _____ vs. 14

- Son of Man _____ vs. 27

- Seal _____ vs. 27

- One Sent _____ vs. 29

- Son _____ vs. 32

- Life Giver _____ vs. 33

- Bread of Life _____ vs. 35

9. The Crowd's Response – vs. 36 _____
_____

Jesus' Two Promises – vs. 37-40

_____
_____

To those who do believe, two promises:

1. Those who come _____ vs. 37
_____
_____
_____

2. Those who do _____ vs. 38-40
_____
_____
_____

Notice that first comes the _____ _____
_____
_____
_____

Then comes _____.

_____

_____

Summary

_____

_____

_____

Jesus preforms _____.

_____

_____

He declares He is:

The _____

The _____

The _____

Some _____ believe and to these He promises:

1. _____

2. _____

Based on this lesson, remember:

Don't _____

_____

_____

When in doubt _____

_____

_____

_____

14. Belief is a Must

Jesus continues His dialogue with the unbelieving crowd and emphasizes that belief is a must if they are to receive the two promises He makes to them. (John 6:41-59)

_____

_____

Intro – Review dialogue between Jesus and the crowd so far:

1. Jesus Returns from Jerusalem
2. Two Miracles
3. The Dialogue
4. The Crowd Tries to Crown Him King
5. Jesus Refuses
6. The People Want Proof
7. Jesus Refuses

Dialogue Continued – 6:41-59

1. The crowd's reaction to Jesus' claims and promises – vs. 41-42

_____

_____

_____

_____

2. Jesus responds to their anger – vs. 43-51

6:43 _____

_____

_____

6:44 _____

_____

_____

6:45 _____

_____

_____

Belief in Jesus is the way to separate those who belong to God and those who don't _____

_____

_____

6:46 _____

_____

_____

Vs. 47-50 – Jesus repeats His previous claims _____

    A. _____

    B. _____

    C. _____

6:51 _____

_____

_____

Jesus lays out a basic message:

    A. _____

    B. _____

    C. _____

Response of the Jews – vs. 52 _____

_____

_____

_____

Jesus calls on them to decide – vs. 53-59 _____

_____

_____

6:53-55 _____

_____

_____

6:56-59 _____

_____

_____

Jesus offers a particular relationship with God through faith.

By faith _____

_____

_____

By faith _____

_____

_____

By faith _____

_____

_____

Faith is expressed in two main ways:

A. _____

_____

Romans 6:3-6; Galatians 3:26-28 _____

_____

_____

Acts 2:38; 22:16; Revelation 1:5 _____

_____

_____

B. _____

_____

_____

_____

Summary

Three concepts from this section:

1. You cannot _____

_____

_____

_____

_____

2. Faith is the _____

_____

_____

_____

_____

3. Genuine faith _____

_____

_____

_____

_____

_____

_____

15. Jesus Knows His Own

In this final section of Jesus' dialogue with an unbelieving crowd, the Lord sets forth the acid test for true discipleship. (John 6:60-71)

_____

_____

Intro – Review sequence in this chapter:

1. Two Miracles _____

2. Proof _____

3. Two Promises _____

4. Hostility _____

5. Faith _____

Dialogue Between Jesus and His Disciples – 6:60-66

_____

_____

_____

1. Reaction of the Disciples – Vs. 60

_____

_____

_____

Note the process of "sifting" _____

_____

_____

2. Jesus responds to Unbelieving Disciples – Vs. 61-65

_____

_____

_____

6:61-62 _____

_____

_____

6:63 – They can't see how a mere "man" can give these things and this is their problem.

_____

_____

_____

They are "caught" in their disbelief _____

_____

_____

6:64-65 _____

_____

_____

Jesus is not teaching "predestination" in this passage. _____

_____

_____

3. Response of the disciples – Vs. 60 _____

_____

_____

Dialogue Between Jesus and the Apostles – vs. 67-70

1. Jesus questions the Apostles – Vs. 67 _____

_____

_____

_____

2. Apostles' response to Jesus – Vs. 68-69 _____

_____

_____

_____

Peter says no for two reasons:

    A.   _____

       _____

    B.   _____

       _____

       _____

3. Jesus' Response to the Apostles' Faith – Vs. 70-71.

_____

_____

_____

_____

Summary

Jesus calls on the people to _____

He declares that those without faith are not _____

Many disciples _____ at this point.

Jesus calls on _____ for their reaction.

Peter declares his _____.

Jesus further proves His _____ by discerning the traitor among them.

_____

_____

_____

_____

Lessons

A. We can't _____ the _____.

_____

_____

_____

_____

_____

B. You can't _____ God.

_____

_____

_____

_____

_____

C. You must _____ and _____

_____

_____

_____

_____

_____

To have _____

_____

_____

_____

_____

16. Jesus in Jerusalem

In this lesson we examine the dialogue that Jesus has with various groups during one of His trips to Jerusalem. (John 7:1-53)

_____

_____

Intro – John's gospel uses "dialogue" to tell the story of Jesus' life:

_____

_____

_____

In chapter 7, Jesus goes to Jerusalem to the Feast of Booths and continues His dialogue with the people.

_____

_____

_____

Dialogue Between Jesus and His Brothers – 7:1-18

_____

_____

Jesus had brothers and sisters (Matthew 12:46-47; Mark 6:3).

_____

_____

7:1-2 _____

_____

_____

7:3-5 _____

_____

_____

7:6-9 _____

_____

_____

7:10-13 _____

_____

_____

Dialogue Between Jesus and the Crowd – vs. 7:14-39

They charge Him with _____ vs. 14-19

_____

_____

_____

Jesus replies with three points:

1. _____

   _____

2. _____

   _____

3. _____

   _____

They charge Him with _____ vs. 20-24

_____

_____

_____

_____

Jesus shows that the miracle does not break the Sabbath. _____

_____

_____

They charge Him with _____ vs. 25-28

_____

_____

They think He is a "pretender" because: _____

_____

_____

Jesus declares _____ vs. 28-29

_____

_____

The Citizens, the Pilgrims and the Leaders are Divided - vs. 30-32

_____

_____

_____

They reiterate their major objections:

- That they or the leaders didn't give credibility, neither should the people.
- That the Messiah would be born in Bethlehem, not Galilee

  (if they would have bothered to ask, Jesus would have told them).

  - They even talk down to Nicodemus when he tries to inject some objectivity into the discussion.
- The episode ends with all the wheels of the cycles still turning:

  - Jesus reveals His divinity with miracles and teaching.
  - Some believe and disbelieve (the conflict continues)
  - Jesus challenges His hearers to convert. (Pert of the steps in evangelism)

Jesus responds to the Leaders - vs. 33-36 _____

_____

_____

Jesus makes a final appeal - vs. 37-39 _____

_____

_____

_____

The Peoples' Final Reaction – vs. 40-53

_____

_____

_____

The Crowds _____

_____

_____

The Temple Guards _____

_____

_____

The Jewish Leaders _____

_____

_____

Note the "cycles" still spinning _____

_____

_____

17. The Pharisees' Attack

More dialogue between Jesus and a woman caught in adultery as well as His denunciation of the hypocritical Jewish leaders. (John 8:1-59)

_____

_____

Intro – Review Chapter 7

_____

_____

Jesus and the Pharisees – 8:1-59

The adulteress woman – 8:1-11

8:1 _____

_____

_____

8:2 _____

_____

_____

8:3-6 _____

_____

_____

8:7-9

In this scene we see the difference between the results of the law and the results of grace.

_____

_____

The Pharisees – 8:12-13

8:12 _____

_____

_____

8:13 _____

_____

8:14-18 _____

_____

Jesus' justification of Himself comes from this knowledge as God, not man. _____

_____

_____

8:19 _____

8:20 _____

8:21 _____

8:22 _____

8:23-24 _____

8:25 _____

8:25b-26 _____

8:27 _____

8:28-29 _____

8:30 _____

_____

Jesus and His <u>New</u> Disciples – 8:31-59

8:31 _____

_____

_____

8:32-33 _____

_____

8:34-38 _____

_____

8:39 _____

_____

8:39b-41 _____

_____

_____

_____

8:41b _____

_____

8:42-47 _____

_____

_____

_____

8:48 _____

_____

8:49-51 _____

_____

8:52-53 _____

_____

8:54-56 _____

_____

_____

8:57 _____

_____

8:58 _____

_____

8:59 _____

_____

_____

_____

Summary

1. The Pharisees _____

_____

_____

2. The Crowd _____

_____

_____

3. The Disciples _____

_____

_____

Lessons

A. Jesus came for _____ not _____.

_____

_____

_____

B. Obedience _____ the men from the boys.

_____

_____

_____

C. Jesus is always _____ His disciples.

_____

_____

_____

18. The Healing and the Attack

Jesus performs a great miracle and is immediately attacked by His enemies in the Jewish leadership. This lesson details the dialogue the Lord has with the Pharisees. (John 9:1-41)

_____

_____

Intro – Review _____

_____

_____

Chapter 8 gives us examples of the cycle of believe and disbelief being carried out.

1. _____

   _____

2. _____

   _____

3. _____

   _____

There are also numerous lessons we can learn from this repeated cycle of events:

A. Jesus came for _____

_____

_____

B. Obedience separates _____

_____

_____

C. Jesus is always _____

_____

_____

_____

_____

Introduction – 9:1-41

_____

_____

This chapter and scene are divided into three sections:

1. Jesus heals the blind man – vs. 1-12 _____

_____

_____

_____

2. The Debate – vs. 13-34 _____

_____

_____

_____

3. Jesus' Declaration – vs. 35-41 _____

_____

_____

_____

The Healing – 9:1-12

_____

_____

_____

9:1-2 _____

_____

_____

9:3-5 _____

_____

_____

9:6-7 _____

_____

_____

9:8-12 _____

_____

_____

_____

The Debate – 9:13-34

_____

_____

_____

The Blind man makes two witnesses:

Witness #1 – vs. 13-23 _____

_____

_____

Witness #2 – vs. 24-34 _____

_____

_____

_____

Jesus Reaffirms His Divinity – 9:35-41

_____

_____

_____

The blind man has a face-to-face meeting with Jesus. _____

_____

_____

9:35-38 _____

_____

_____

_____

9:39-41 _____

_____

_____

_____

Summary

This is only the middle part of a longer section where the Lord is dealing with the Pharisees.

_____

_____

_____

_____

_____

_____

_____

_____

_____

19. Jesus Rebukes the Jewish Leaders

The parable of the Good Shepherd points to both the failings of the Jewish leadership and the eventual redemptive work of the true leader and shepherd of Israel. (John 10:1-42)

_____

_____

Intro – Review of Events:

- Jesus challenged by His family
- Teaches at Jerusalem during "Booths"
- Causes division
- Pharisees set a trap
- More division
- Disciples are "sifted"
- Heals a blind man
- Conflict with leaders
- Reveals Himself to the blind man
- Denounces Jewish leaders

_____

_____

_____

Parable of the Good Shepherd – 10:1-21

_____

_____

_____

This parable follows naturally after Jesus' condemnation of _____.

_____

_____

_____

Sheep folds:

    A. Open type _____

_____

_____

    B. Closed type _____

_____

_____

10:1-2_____

_____

_____

10:3-5 _____

_____

_____

10:6 _____

_____

_____

Explanation of Parable – vs. 7-21

10:7-10 _____

_____

_____

10:11-13 _____

_____

_____

10:14-18 – Jesus says the following about the "Good Shepherd"

1. The Good Shepherd _____ His sheep.

2. The Good Shepherd will _____ for His sheep.

3. The Good Shepherd will bring _____ into the fold.

_____

_____

_____

10:19-21 _____

_____

_____

_____

Jesus Declares His Divinity Without a Parable – vs. 22-42

_____

_____

_____

Feast of "Dedication" _____

_____

_____

10:22-24 _____

_____

_____

10:25-31

1. _____

2. _____

3. _____

10:32 _____

_____

_____

10:33 _____

_____

_____

10:34-38 _____

_____

_____

10:39 _____

_____

_____

10:40-42 _____

_____

_____

20. The Resurrection of Lazarus

The death and resurrection of Lazarus are viewed from the eyes of the principal characters who witnessed this great miracle by Jesus.
(John 11:1-57)

_____

_____

Intro – Chapter 11 begins a new phase in Jesus' ministry.

_____

_____

With this miracle Jesus will:

- o End _____.
- o Prove _____.
- o Provide _____.

The Death and Resurrection of Lazarus

11:1-6 _____

_____

_____

John divides the story into four parts showing how different people react to this miracle.

1. The Apostles – vs. 7-46

11:7-8 _____

_____

_____

11:9-10 _____

_____

_____

11:11-12 _____

_____

_____

11:13-15 _____

_____

_____

11:16 _____

_____

_____

2. Martha

11:17 _____

_____

_____

11:18-22 _____

_____

_____

11:23 _____

_____

_____

11:24 _____

_____

_____

11:25-26 _____

_____

_____

11:27 _____

_____

_____

Note her response:

- Yes _____
- Lord _____
- Believe _____
- Christ _____
- Son of God _____
- Comes into the world _____

3. Mary

11:28-31 _____

_____

_____

11:32-33a _____

_____

_____

11:33b-37 _____

_____

_____

4. Jesus

11:38-40 _____

_____

_____

11:41-42 _____

_____

_____

11:43-44 _____

_____

_____

11:45-46 _____

_____

_____

The Conspiracy – vs. 47-57

11:47-48 _____

_____

_____

11:49-53 _____

_____

_____

11:54-57 _____

_____

_____

21. Reaction to Lazarus' Resurrection

In this section John describes the reaction that various people had to Lazarus' miraculous resurrection. (John 12:1-50)

_____

_____

Intro – First 11 chapters span several years, last ten chapters compress time.

_____

_____

Reactions To Lazarus' Resurrection: 12:1-26

_____

_____

1. Mary, the Sister to Lazarus – vs. 1-3

_____

_____

Bethany was near Jerusalem and Jesus stayed there often. _____

_____

_____

Exposing one's hair in mixed company was not done by women of that day. _____

_____

_____

2. Judas Iscariot – vs. 4-8

_____

_____

Judas could have objected on several grounds:

   1. _____

_____

   2. _____

_____

He accuses Jesus of _____

_____

_____

Judas' reaction to the miracle was to continue to have _____

_____

_____

Jesus defends Mary's actions:

- Her faith _____

_____

- The poor _____

_____

- His death _____

_____

3. The Jewish Leaders – vs. 9-11

_____

_____

The leaders are on the wrong side _____

_____

_____

4. The Multitudes – vs. 12-19

_____

_____

They were acknowledging Him as a glorious leader. _____

_____

_____

_____

5. The Gentiles (Greeks) – vs. 20-26

The leaders were afraid of losing their power and hated the idea that Gentiles would mix with the Jews. _____

_____

_____

_____

Jesus uses the request of the Greeks to declare two events.

- The Passion _____

_____

_____

- The Choice _____

_____

_____

The Cycle Continues – vs. 27-50

_____

_____

The familiar cycle of belief and disbelief continues. _____

_____

_____

12:27-36 – Four voices mingled:

1. Jesus _____

_____

_____

2. God the Father _____

_____

_____

3. The Multitudes _____

_____

_____

4. John _____

_____

_____

The Warning

A final warning to those who have seen the miracles and heard the words.

1. Reject Me and _____

_____

_____

_____

_____

2. The basis for judgement _____

_____

_____

_____

_____

As it was then, so it is today _____

_____

_____

_____

_____

_____

22. The Last Supper

The final hours of Jesus' life begin with the Passover meal with His Apostles where He will demonstrate both His power and humility. (John 13:1-30)

_____

_____

Intro – Review the objectives of "cycles":

1. Clarity _____

   _____

   _____

2. Proof _____

   _____

   _____

3. Record _____

   _____

   _____

The Passover Meal – Background

1. The Passover Feast _____

_____

_____

Each element of the meal had significance:

A. The Lamb _____

   _____

B. The Herbs _____

   _____

C. The Unleavened bread _____

   _____

D. The Wine _____

   _____

   _____

2. The removal of "leaven" _____

_____

_____

3. The meal was "presided" over by the father or a leader. _____

_____

_____

Jesus and the Passover – 13:1-30

_____

_____

Jesus does two important things for His Apostles:

1. He washes their feet _____

_____

_____

13:1-5 _____

_____

_____

13:6-11 _____

_____

_____

13:12-17 _____

_____

_____

13:18-20 _____

_____

_____

2. He reveals the Traitor _____

_____

_____

13:21-30 – Imagine the scene:

Simon Peter	⎡ ⎤	John
Thomas		Jesus
Nathaniel		Judas
Philip	⎣_____⎦	Simon Zelotes

Judas Alpheus James Alpheus Andrew James Zebedee Matthew

_____

_____

_____

_____

John gives three important facts:

1. Peter's feet were washed _____.

2. Peter had to _____ get John's attention.

3. Jesus spoke and handed the morsel _____ to _____.

"Satan entering Judas" _____

_____

_____

_____

Summary

Even though the Lord's supper is not described here, this passage teaches similar lessons:

Lesson #1 – A Servant _____

_____

_____

_____

_____

_____

Lesson #2 – A Servant _____

_____

_____

_____

_____

_____

23. Jesus' Final Teaching - Part 1

John recounts four dialogues that Jesus has with different apostles after they had shared the Passover meal. (John 13:31-14:31)

_____

_____

Intro – Jesus and the Apostles are in the Upper Room.

_____

_____

Jesus' Final Teaching and Encouragement

This is the main body of teaching and encouragement to His Apostles before the Lord's death.

_____

_____

Dialogue #1 – Jesus and Peter – 13:31-35

13:31-33 – The cycle of events leading to the cross begins with Judas' departure.

_____

_____

Jesus declares that even the cross is a source of glory for Him.

_____

_____

13:34-35 – The commandment to "Love" is not new but the reason and manner is.

A. _____

B. _____

C. _____

13:36 _____

_____

_____

13:37-38 – Peter makes a rash statement. _____

_____

_____

_____

Dialogue #2 – Jesus and Thomas – 14:1-6

14:1-4 – The evening has become quite depressing. _____

_____

_____

14:5 – Thomas still doesn't understand. _____

_____

_____

14:6 – Jesus answers in a beautiful & concise manner.

    A. _____

    B. _____

    C. _____

Dialogue #3 – Philip – 14:7-15

14:7 – Jesus expands on a previous thought. _____

_____

_____

14:8 – Philip only understands in part. _____

_____

_____

14:9-15 – Jesus convinces Philip further:

A. _____

_____

B. _____

_____

C. _____

_____

Dialogue #4 – Judas (Thaddeus) – 14:16-24

_____

_____

14:16-21 – Jesus builds yet another idea upon the one He had just given in response to Philip.

_____

_____

They will recognize the Spirit because He will lead them to the truth, the same truth originally given them by Jesus. _____

_____

_____

God "manifests" Himself to the believer through:

1. _____

_____

_____

2. _____

_____

_____

3. _____

_____

_____

14:22 _____

_____

_____

_____

14:23-24 – Jesus answers him that the revelation of the Father for anyone is based on the acceptance of the Son. _____

_____

_____

_____

_____

Summary

Jesus has answered their final questions and will summarize His response to them in this section.

1. He reviews _____ vs. 25-27

   _____

   _____

   _____

2. He reminds _____ vs. 28-31

   _____

   _____

   _____

24. Jesus' Final Teaching - Part 2

Jesus continues teaching and encouraging His disciples before He is betrayed by Judas. (John 15:1-27)

_____

_____

Intro – Jesus prepared His Apostles for His departure in several ways:

1. _____

2. _____

3. _____

4. _____

Jesus' Teaching and Encouragements – Chapter 15

_____

_____

_____

In Chapter 15 Jesus encourages His Apostles to persevere in many areas:

1. They should _____ **vs. 15:1-11**

_____

_____

15:1-2 _____

_____

_____

In the summary statement Jesus explains four ideas:

A. _____

B. _____

C. _____

D. _____

15:3-12 – In case the Apostles doubt their own condition, Jesus reassures them.

_____

_____

_____

The Lord mentions seven details concerning the relationship between the vine, the vinedresser, and the branch:

1. _____

2. _____

3. _____

4. _____

5. _____

6. _____

7. _____

2. They should _____ **vs. 12-17**

_____

_____

15:12-13 _____

_____

_____

15:14-15 _____

_____

_____

15:16-17 – Their friendship has conditions. _____

_____

_____

Jesus' conditions for friendship are things that will contribute to the friendship:

- Continued _____
  _____

- Continued _____
  _____

- Continued _____
  _____

3. They should _____ vs. 18-27

_____

_____

Jesus prepared them for His final departure. _____

_____

_____

15:18-20 _____

_____

_____

He warns them of five things:

    A. The world _____

      _____

    B. The world _____

      _____

    C. The world _____

      _____

    D. The world _____

      _____

    E. The world _____

      _____

15:21 _____

_____

_____

15:22-25 – Jesus tells them that rejections of the Father is without excuse. Why?

_____

_____

_____

15:26-27 _____

_____

_____

_____

Jesus prepares them by encouraging them to continue in: _____

_____

_____

_____

_____

_____

_____

25. Jesus' Final Teaching - Part 3

In this section of the Lord's final teaching, He encourages the Apostles as He reviews with them what will take place in the near future. (John 16:1-33)

_____

_____

Intro – Review _____

_____

_____

The Warning – 16:1-4

16:1 – The "things" He refers to are: _____

_____

_____

16:2 _____

_____

_____

16:3_____

_____

_____

16:4_____

_____

_____

Four Promises

Promise #1 _____vs. 5-15

_____

_____

Condition of the Holy Spirit's coming – vs. 5-7 _____

_____

_____

The work of the Holy Spirit. – vs. 8-11 _____

_____

_____

The Spirit will convict the world of:

1. _____

_____

2. _____

_____

3. _____

_____

The way the Holy Spirit will work

_____

_____

16:12 _____

_____

16:13 _____

_____

16:14 _____

_____

16:15 _____

_____

Promise #2 _____ vs. 16-22

_____

_____

16:16 _____

_____

_____

16:17-18 _____

_____

_____

16:19-20 _____

_____

_____

16:21-22 _____

_____

_____

_____

Promise #3 _____ vs. 23-24

_____

_____

_____

_____

_____

_____

Promise #4 _____ **vs. 25-33**

_____

_____

16:25-28 _____

_____

_____

16:29-30 _____

_____

_____

16:31-33 _____

_____

_____

Summary

As His time with the Apostles draws to a close Jesus promises them four things:

1. _____

2. _____

3. _____

4. _____

_____

_____

_____

_____

_____

26. Jesus' Final Teaching - Part 4

In this last portion of Jesus' time with the Apostles before His death, the Lord makes what has been referred to as His "High Priestly" prayer where He prays for Himself, the Apostles and future generation of Christians. (John 17:1-26)

_____

_____

Intro – The same cycle appears throughout John:

1. _____

2. _____

3. _____

Review of teaching in "upper" room: _____

_____

_____

The High Priestly Prayer

David Chytraeus – 16th century _____

_____

_____

The difference between Jesus and the High Priest:

- Jesus did not need _____

- Jesus did not offer _____

- Jesus would relate _____

This section can be divided into three sections:

- Prayer for _____ vs. 1-5

- Prayer for _____ vs. 6-19

- Prayer for _____ vs. 20-26

1. Jesus' Prayer for Himself – vs. 1-5

_____

_____

17:1 _____

_____

The "hour" is the time for all things to be fulfilled. _____

_____

_____

Jesus' glorification is tied to His resurrection:

- Resurrection confirms _____ John 20:31
- Resurrection confirms _____ John 20:31
- Resurrection confirms _____ Colossians 1:16

The Father is glorified by the resurrection:

- Reveals His _____ Romans 1:4
- Reveals His _____ Romans 3:21-26
- Reveals His _____ Romans 5:8

_____

_____

17:2-3 _____

_____

_____

17:4-5 _____

_____

_____

2. Jesus' Prayer for the Apostles – vs. 6-19

_____

_____

_____

_____

How Jesus feels about His Apostles – vs. 6-10 _____

_____

_____

What Jesus wants from His Apostles – vs. 11-19 _____

_____

_____

_____

To sanctify means to "Set Apart" _____

_____

_____

_____

_____

3. Jesus' Prayer for Future Disciples – vs. 20-26

_____

_____

_____

17:20-21 – He prays that the growth & unity of the church will provide an ongoing witness to an unbelieving world. _____

_____

_____

17:22-23 _____

_____

_____

_____

17:24-26 _____

_____

_____

_____

Summary

_____

_____

_____

_____

_____

_____

27. The Passion - Part 1

John begins to describe the events that led up to
Jesus' torture and crucifixion. (John 18:1-38a)

_____

_____

Intro – Jesus prayed for several things in the prayer that we studied last week:

1. He promised _____
2. He prays that _____
3. He expresses _____
4. He prays that _____

Judas' Betrayal – 18:1-11

18:1-2 – They leave the upper room and cross the valley of Kidron _____

_____

_____

18:3-9 – The arrest _____

_____

_____

18:10-11 – Peter's attack _____

_____

_____

Jesus Before the Priests – vs. 12-27

There were three sessions with the Jewish leaders before going on to Pilate:

1. Annas _____
2. Caiaphas _____
3. Caiaphas _____
4. Pilate _____

18:12-14 _____

_____

18:15-18 _____

_____

18:19-24 – Annas is searching for a charge. _____

_____

18:25-27 – Back in the courtyard with Peter. _____

_____

Jesus Before Pilate – vs. 28-38a

John does not describe any of the trials before Caiaphas

(Matthew 26:59-68; Mark 14:55-65; Luke 22:66-71)

_____

_____

18:28-32 _____

_____

_____

The Jews reveal their "true" intent, the death penalty. _____

_____

_____

18:33-38a – Pilate takes custody of Jesus when he realizes this case may require an execution.

_____

_____

Jesus continues the "cycle" in declaring His divinity _____

_____

_____

Pilate's response is sad because it falls short by one word. _____

_____

_____

28. The Passion - Part 2

This lesson examines the various trials and leaders Jesus faced before He is ultimately condemned to the cross. John also provides a brief description of the scene at the crucifixion. (John 18:38b-19:30)

_____

_____

Intro – Review trial appearances by Jesus: _____

_____

_____

Trial Before Pilate Continued – 18:38-19:16

_____

_____

_____

18:38-40 – Pilate believes Jesus is innocent of the charges.

_____

_____

_____

Information on Herod the Tetrarch.

_____

_____

_____

Pilate is confident that the people will choose Jesus over Barabbas.

_____

_____

_____

19:1-5 – Pilate gives orders to torture Jesus

_____

_____

_____

Pilate has three goals:

1. _____

2. _____

3. _____

19:6-11 – The crowd cries out for crucifixion. _____

_____

_____

_____

Pilate is frightened by who Jesus might be. _____

_____

_____

_____

_____

Jesus tells Pilate two things:

1. _____

2. _____

19:12-16 – The Jews focus on Pilate's vulnerability _____

_____

_____

_____

The Jews give Pilate what he needs to carry out the execution:

1. A charge _____

2. A law _____

3. Motivation _____

4. A Promise _____

_____

_____

_____

The Crucifixion – vs. 17-30

_____

_____

_____

19:17-22 – John focuses on Jesus' identity. _____

_____

_____

_____

19:23-27 – Jewish men wore five pieces of clothing. _____

_____

_____

_____

The soldiers fulfill a prophecy in Psalm 22:18. _____

_____

_____

_____

_____

Note the three Mary's at the scene:

- _____
- _____
- _____

19:28-30 – All means all things given by _____ and spoken of in the _____.

_____
_____
_____

Jesus controlled His death because:

_____
_____
_____

_____
_____
_____

29. Death / Burial / Resurrection

The apostle John provides the details surrounding the actual burial of Christ as well as the flow of events immediately after Jesus' resurrection. (John 19:31-20:18)

_____

_____

Intro – John focuses much attention on Jesus' encounter with Pilate.

_____

_____

_____

Death and Burial – vs. 30-42

John spends little time on the actual crucifixion and more on people's reaction to it.

_____

_____

A. Jesus' Death – vs. 30-37

19:30 – John claims three things with the death of Jesus.

    A. It was _____

    B. It was _____

    C. He was _____

19:31-34 – The Jewish law required those executed to be removed before sundown to avoid polluting the land. _____

_____

_____

19:35-37 – Even Jesus' lifeless body serves to promote faith.

_____

_____

B. Jesus' Burial – vs. 38-42

After the crucifixion John introduces the characters who will bury Jesus.

19:38 – Joseph of Arimathea _____

_____

_____

_____

19:39 – Nicodemus _____

_____

_____

19:40-42 – The burial location _____

_____

_____

The Resurrection – vs. 20:1-18

None of the gospel writers describe the actual resurrection, only the signs pointing to it.

_____

_____

_____

20:1-2 – The women arrive before Joseph or Nicodemus _____

_____

_____

_____

20:3-10 – Peter and John come to the tomb to verify the women's account. _____

_____

_____

_____

The scene at the tomb provides true signs of resurrection:

1. The bandages _____

_____

_____

2. The face cloth _____

_____

_____

Peter and John's coming to faith is painful. _____

_____

_____

_____

20:11-13 – The scene shifts back to Mary _____

_____

_____

_____

20:14-15 – Jesus appears to Mary _____

_____

_____

_____

20:16-18 – Mary comes to see _____

_____

_____

_____

_____

Jesus' response to her is not "harsh" _____

_____

_____

_____

_____

In His appearance to Mary we see two things:

1. _____

_____

_____

_____

2. _____

_____

_____

_____

30. Appearances to the Apostles

In this lesson, we will review the 11 recorded appearances of Jesus after His resurrection and final ascension into heaven. (John 20:19-21:25)

_____

_____

Intro – John examines the faith of those who came in contact with Jesus at the point of His death, burial and resurrection.

_____

_____

Three Appearances to the Apostles – 20:19-21:25

The Bible records at least 11 appearances by the resurrected Jesus:

1. _____ Mk.16:9-11; Jn. 20:11-18
2. _____ Mt. 28:8-10; Mk. 16:8, Lk. 24:9-11
3. _____ Lk. 24:34; I Cor. 15:5
4. _____ Lk. 24:34
5. _____ Mk. 16:14; Lk. 24:36; Jn 20:19-23
6. _____ Jn. 20:24-29
7. _____ Jn. 21:1-24
8. _____ Mt. 28:16-20; Mk. 16:15-18
9. _____ I Cor. 15:7
10. _____ Mk. 16:19; Lk. 24:50-53, Acts 1:9-12
11. _____ I Cor. 15:8

John describes 4 of the appearances; one to Mary Magdalene and three to the Apostles as a group.

Jesus Appears to the Apostles Without Thomas – 20:19-23

20:19-20 _____

_____

_____

20:21-23 – In these verses Jesus does three important things:

1. He commissions them _____

_____

_____

_____

2. He gives them _____

_____

_____

_____

3. He grants them _____

_____

_____

_____

Appearance to Apostles with Thomas – vs. 24-29

20:24-25 _____

_____

_____

_____

20:26-29 _____

_____

_____

_____

Conclusion and Summary #1 – 20:30-31

20:30-31 _____

_____

_____

Appearance to Apostles by the Sea – 21:1-24

_____

_____

Background information on this chapter _____

_____

_____

21:1 _____

_____

21:2-3 _____

_____

21:4-6 _____

_____

21:7-8 _____

_____

21:9-11 _____

_____

21:12-14 _____

_____

21:15-17 _____

_____

_____

Jesus publicly restores Peter by asking him three questions:

Question #1 _____

_____

Answer #1 _____

_____

Question #2 _____

_____

Answer #2 _____

_____

Question #3 _____

_____

Answer #3 _____

_____

21:18-24 _____

_____

_____

_____

Conclusion and Summary #2 – 21:25

_____

_____

_____

_____

_____

_____

_____

31. Gospel of John Review

A final look at the entire gospel and summary of its main theme. This lesson also includes a review test with questions over the entire book.

1. Match the correct word with the correct statement:

A. People who were considered as "half breeds" by the Jews _____

B. The process of bringing people to Christ _____

C. One of the men who buried Jesus _____

D. The person Jesus appeared to first after His resurrection. _____

E. A Greek term referring to a ruler who was responsible for one quarter

of a Roman Province. _____

F. The man who found Jesus innocent three times. _____

G. The father-in-law of the ruling high priest when Jesus was tried. _____

H. The term used to describe Jesus' lengthy prayer
   on the night of His betrayal _____

I. The condition required for the Holy Spirit's coming. _____

J. What Jesus & the Apostles were doing the night of His betrayal. _____

1. Pilate	7.	High Priestly Prayer
2. Tetrarch	8.	Jesus' death
3. Samaritans	9.	Mary Magdalene
4. Personal Evangelism	10.	Joseph
5. Annas	11.	Peter
6. Passover	12.	Governor
	13.	Caiaphas

2. Fill in the blanks with the correct word in the following sentences:

A. The sub-title of this study in the gospel of John has been,

   Jesus the _____ /_____.

B. The reoccurring themes in John's book were referred

   to as _____ of belief or disbelief.

C. Jesus provided proof of His divinity through His _____.

D. The Lord's first miracle occurred at _____.

E. John was from the northern part of Israel near the sea of _____.

F. Jesus often stayed with His friends, Mary, Martha

   and Lazarus who lived in _____.

G. _____ was the ruling high priest at Jesus' trial.

H. The Bible records a total of _____ appearances by Jesus after His resurrection.

I. Jesus promised the Apostles that He would send them the _____ who would

   lead them to all _____.

3. Mark these statements as True or False:

☐ True ☐ False   A. John was the son of a wealthy fisherman.

☐ True ☐ False   B. Jesus' miracles were done to create respect for God in the people.

☐ True ☐ False   C. John is the only gospel writer to record all three of Jesus' appearances to the Apostles after His resurrection.

☐ True ☐ False   D. The "Follow-Through" of faith is obedience.

☐ True ☐ False

    E. John has carefully recorded all that Jesus said and did.

☐ True ☐ False

    F. Jesus did not have to be baptized because He was the Son of God.

☐ True ☐ False

    G. Jesus' last public miracle was the feeding of the 5,000.

☐ True ☐ False

    H. The beginning of John's gospel is usually referred to as the "Introduction."

☐ True ☐ False

    I. The purpose of John's gospel is that his readers will respect Jesus.

☐ True ☐ False

    J. This is the best textual Bible class you have ever had.

Total Points – 30

Your Score _____

BibleTalk.tv is an Internet Mission Work.

We provide video and textual Bible teaching material on our website and mobile apps for free. We enable churches and individuals all over the world to have access to high quality Bible materials for personal growth, group study or for teaching in their classes.

The goal of this mission work is to spread the gospel to the greatest number of people using the latest technology available. For the first time in history, it is becoming possible to preach the gospel to the entire world at once. BibleTalk.tv is an effort to preach the gospel to all nations every day until Jesus returns.

The Choctaw Church of Christ in Oklahoma City is the sponsoring congregation for this work and provides the oversight for the BibleTalk.tv ministry team. If you would like information on how you can support this ministry, please go to the link provided below.

bibletalk.tv/support

"

BibleTalk.tv is one of the **most-prolific uploaders** on Amazon Prime Video with more videos than any major Hollywood studio except Paramount Pictures.

THE WALL STREET JOURNAL.